How To Start a Restaurant without Losing your Shirt

By Brian Cliette
© 2014 Bull City Publishing
Duplication prohibited

Visit us at Bullcitypublishing.com **for more great titles!**

TABLE OF CONTENT

Chapter 1

Introduction

"Victory becomes, to some degree, a state of mind. Knowing ourselves superior to the anxieties, troubles, and worries which obsess us, we are superior to them." - **Basil King**

How can I start a restaurant? If you've asked yourself that question, this ebook is for you!

The fact that you even chose to buy this book shows that you have some commitment to starting a restaurant. That commitment will be the ingredient that helps you conquer the challenges facing any entrepreneur.

You may feel unqualified to start a restaurant. That is not true! Anyone who has the drive to make it work can accomplish this goal. In fact, starting a restaurant is a great business move. You do not have to have a college degree to make your dining establishment great. You don't have to have endless funds. You don't even have to know how to cook! Starting a restaurant simply demands hard work and an understanding of the steps that must be taken to get the business up and running.

Nothing should keep you from starting a restaurant if that is your dream. The fear of an uncertain economy, the lack of funds you may face at first, the long hours you will put in – all of these things are simply challenges that you can overcome. The desire you have to make this happen is what will give you the courage to open the doors of your restaurant!

Everyone who dreams of beginning their own restaurant wonders how they will reach that goal. Some people never begin because they feel they don't know enough about how to proceed. This ebook will guide you through the many aspects of restauranting that you need to know about in order to be successful in your quest. It won't bog you down with unimportant details or confuse you with unfamiliar jargon. Instead, it will be your teacher, showing you how to put your business together one piece at a time.

Many of the steps covered here are going to demand a commitment of time. They may even sound a little bit intimidating at first. Don't let that get in your way. The goal of this ebook is to help you conquer those worries by showing you the simple way to get those tasks accomplished. At the end of this ebook, you should feel very comfortable doing any of the steps required to start your own restaurant.

Next, in Chapter 2, you will be encouraged to ask if starting a restaurant is really right for you. You will learn about the hard work and varied tasks involved in running a restaurant. You will also read about five restaurant myths that you have probably heard before! This section will demystify the restaurant business and tell you the truth about those myths. If you have ever wondered about why some restaurants fail, the simple answer is that the owner had the wrong outlook to begin with! Our section on myths will help you think about your own view of the restaurant industry and your role in it.

By the end of the chapter, you will have an idea of what it is really like to be a restaurant owner. That's the first step toward preparing to run your own restaurant, so the final section gives you a detailed look at what is involved in a restaurant owner's life.

In chapter 3, you will get the scoop on designing your restaurant. Whether you want to run a franchise restaurant or create one from scratch, you will benefit from the insights offered. The chapter will describe the pros and cons of both franchise and independent restaurants so you can make an informed decision on which kind you want to own.

For the franchisee, there is a section on how to get your franchise restaurant off to a running start. You will learn about the costs involved in buying a franchise, and even about some fees you may not be expecting. For instance, many franchises charge you an automatic fee in order to finance their marketing. You will need to be aware of these hidden costs before purchasing a franchise.

You'll also learn about the different kinds of restaurants, from cafés to fine dining. The guide we have put together will offer you clear definitions on what people expect from certain types of restaurant. This may even be the place to go if you are feeling stumped about the theme of your restaurant!

Chapter 4, *Location, Location, Location*, is about finding the place where your restaurant can shine. You will need to have a clear idea of what kind of restaurant you are going to be running before you can pick out the right area. This chapter will guide you through the steps of choosing a location and researching the population.

There is also a section on negotiating a lease, which you should read before you sign on the dotted line! The suggestions found in this section can assist you in getting the best deal possible. For instance, did you know that some landlords will let you have the first few months at no cost? They do this to give you time to set up your restaurant because they are hoping the new business will add to their property value. This is only one of the many insights offered in the lease section.

Most people are frightened by the thought of writing a business plan, but this necessary task does not have to be scary or difficult! In Chapter 5, you will learn the basic business plan format that you should use. This will make your business plan look so much more professional than if it was simply thrown together! Bankers and other investors will expect to see certain aspects of the business addressed before they will feel comfortable giving you money.

You will also find Chapter 5 helpful as you learn how to make more or less accurate financial projections. These numbers will be vital to your business as it grows. You can look at them over the months and see if your real life profit matches up with the projection. If the numbers don't go together, it will indicate that you need to modify your business practices.

Finally, you will learn about budgeting your restaurant. This is a crucial part of running any business, and a restaurant is no different. Our friendly guide will help you see all the places where money will be coming in and going out so you can make a realistic budget.

Once you have gotten comfortable thinking about the budget, you will move on to Chapter 6, which will give you insight into refining your restaurant concept. With the wide variety of restaurant types to choose from, this section may help clear up some of the categories. This will help you get your restaurant's finished concept firmly in mind so you can move forward with designing it in the real world.

The next section is one offers some of the most valuable advice in Chapter 6, and it is all about writing the menu! This is where most restaurants stand or fall. With the tips and tricks included in this section, you can feel confident that your menu is balanced and intriguing. No matter what kind of restaurant you own, some of the principles of menu writing remain the same: offer a range of prices, put something familiar or classic on the menu, and target your demographic.

The next three sections deal with pricing your menu, designing its appearance, and a few other helpful hints. Many new restaurant owners tend to worry about menu prices. It can be hard to guess how much people will pay, but this ebook was written to take the guesswork out of your new restaurant! You will learn the hard and fast ways to find a price that customers are willing to pay and that you will profit from.

Menu design can be fun and rewarding, but there are a few pitfalls that you should avoid. Our section on creating the look of your menu will help you put together the right combination of fonts, colors, and styles. Your guests should get a feel for the kind of food to expect from looking at the menu, and this section will give you the tools to make that a reality.

In Chapter 7, you will learn about the realities of running your own restaurant. The guidance offered on how to run the business smoothly may prove invaluable! The first section will give you an overview of the restaurant jobs that must be filled, from the dishwasher to the chef. Each of these jobs is described and outlined for your convenience.

The two sections that follow will give you a few tips on hiring for the front of the house (the dining area) and the back of the house (the kitchen, business office, and any other behind-the-scenes area). Each staff position calls for a certain type of person, and these sections will help you picture who you want to hire.

You will also learn about equipping your restaurant. There are a number of ways to save when outfitting your business, and this section will give you a few examples. The next section will explain the necessity of having a point of sale (POS) system in place before you open for business. The need for one of these automated tracking systems will become more obvious as the number of clients increases!

The final section of Chapter 7 will give you insider knowledge on why it is wise to lease your equipment instead of buying it. This step alone can save you thousands of dollars at the beginning of your restaurant, and it will continue to save you money over the years. Just knowing that you are not responsible for repairs when leased items break can take a load of worry off your shoulders.

Chapter 8 is the conclusion, and it offers a helpful summary of the most important information contained in the book and even has bonus materials.

You'll find some pep talk in there, as well, just in case the amount of information has seemed a bit overwhelming. The goal of this ebook is to help you succeed and create the restaurant you have always wanted to run.

In the rest of this ebook, you will find insider advice, money-saving tips, and general guidelines to follow as you start your restaurant. Look at this ebook as a guide, not a rulebook. If you find that some piece of advice doesn't fit in with your vision of the finished restaurant, don't hesitate to find a different way. However, keep in mind that much of the information you will get here comes from those who have experience running their own restaurant.

If you're wondering if you can really start a restaurant, the answer is yes! If you have the desire and the commitment to make it work, you can start the restaurant of your dreams. This ebook will show you how.

Chapter 2

How to Get Started Deciding if Owning a Restaurant is Right for You

*"We will often find compensation if we think more of what life has given us and less about what life has taken away." - **William Barclay***

It is easy to fantasize about owning your own restaurant. Popular television shows make it look fun and maybe even simple. You have probably daydreamed about the décor and the menu in your future restaurant. However, there are many factors involved in deciding if owning a restaurant fits in with your goals and life!

To begin with, you will need to look into the financial aspect of starting up a restaurant. How much capital do you have already? If you don't have enough to cover the startup costs, how will you make up the difference? Loans can sometimes be the only feasible option for new business owners, and a restaurant is just that – a business.

You will also have to decide what type of restaurant you wish to have. Franchise restaurants do not allow you the creativity you would have with a brand new restaurant, but they do have the advantage of being well known and easy to run. On the other hand, a unique restaurant built from the ground up can let you create an exciting new dining experience for your customers.

Finally, do you have the guts to take risks? In the restaurant business, you will be working long hours and starting something new in the area, whether it is a franchise or your personal brand of restaurant. Running a restaurant can be a demanding job, and you will have to possess lots of confidence in yourself and your business plan in order to succeed.

A good first step would be to write down the goals you have for your restaurant. If you end up needing to look into a loan or other funding options, this business plan can help you win people over to your cause. Let's find out if owning a restaurant is right for you!

Is Owning a Restaurant Right for You?

Are you the kind of person who will enjoy running your own restaurant? There are a few indicators that can help you decide if this is the career you are truly meant for. While there are no hard and fast rules about who can make it as a restaurant owner, there are a couple of traits many successful owners share.

How well can you take the heat? A restaurant can be a very stressful place, and if you actually run the show, it can be even more demanding. The staff is going to be looking to you as the leader, and you will be responsible for the food, the décor, the budget – literally everything that goes on in your business.

You will also need to be able to handle a number of issues at once! Multitaskers are great at this sort of job, because a restaurant requires you to be available to help when anything goes wrong. You must be flexible enough to do a variety of tasks and reach outside of your comfort zone.

You will also be spending a good deal of time at your restaurant on Fridays, Saturdays, and Sundays! These are the days when most people want to kick back and let someone else cook for them, and your restaurant is where they will look for a great weekend meal. Early mornings and late nights add to the hours you'll need to spend on the job.

Most restaurant owners relish the opportunity to meet new people. Serving others is what restaurants are all about, and you, as the owner, will have to anticipate the needs of your guests. They are paying your bills, and they want to have an excellent experience. Of course, a good owner enjoys talking with customers and finding out what may need improvement in the restaurant.

Now, if all this hasn't scared you off, then you may just have what it takes to successfully run a restaurant of your own. Next, we'll investigate Five Restaurant Myths.

Five Restaurant Myths

Let's examine some of the myths that people think of when they consider owning a restaurant. First of all, the myth of **It Will Be So Much Fun**. Everyone tends to picture the restaurant owner as a person who just goofs off and enjoys watching the money roll in, while the staff keeps the restaurant going. The truth is that there is far more hard work involved in the restaurant biz than there is fun. This is not a job where you can show up when you feel like it! It will require a huge investment of time, particularly when you are first starting out.

Our next myth is that **My Buddies Can Chill At the Restaurant**. This is a terrible reason to think about owning a restaurant. In fact, it doesn't even make sense. Your friends may enjoy popping by to get some free food once in a while, but they probably won't see much of you if you are truly running a business.

The number three myth is that **Restaurant Owners Are Celebrities**. While it's true that there are quite a number of chefs who star in network television shows, it is equally true that most chefs never achieve that type of success. However, success does not have to be defined by how many people know your name! Your restaurant's success is your success.

Some people believe the myth that **A Restaurant is a Money Machine**. There are huge financial demands on restaurants, from licensing laws and fees to renting a facility to paying your employees.

Often, the restaurant owner is the first person to go without a check when times are tough.

Finally, we confront the myth that **I Love Cooking and That's Reason Enough**. No, it isn't! You may thoroughly enjoy cooking, but that will not be the only thing you have to do as a restaurant owner. Actually, you may find that you have less time to cook than you had before you opened the restaurant. Make sure that you are opening a restaurant because it is your dream, not because you like to whip up recipes for your friends.

What It's Really Like Being a Restaurant Owner

You probably will face a number of challenges as a restaurant owner. As mentioned before, weekends will be workdays now. Depending on when your restaurant opens, you may find yourself running from dawn until late in the evening. Be aware that you will need to find a way to spend time with your family and friends, and that this won't always be easy.

Many restaurant owners end up doing a little bit of everything, just because they are the owners and have the final say in what happens in a given situation. Hiring and firing rests on your shoulders, and you will also have to deal with the inevitable telemarketing calls that come in offering you all kinds of appliances and kitchen accessories.

You will also need to be ready to go over any discrepancies in the payroll or the tips garnered by the wait staff. It is your job to make sure that everyone gets a paycheck, even if you have to short yourself on occasion. The best decision you can make as a new restaurant owner is to delegate specific jobs to your employees so they know what is expected of them – and so you can focus on managing the restaurant!

Get ready to go over the details of the menu with your chef and kitchen staff, and be flexible enough to make changes seasonally. Keeping your offerings fresh can lead to more repeat customers as you serve up something that is interesting and different!

You'll also have to be an interior decorator, sometimes on a strict budget!

As the owner, you do get one benefit that nobody else can share: the satisfaction of watching *your* restaurant become successful. You take on the responsibilities, but you also get to feel a sense of accomplishment as your reward!

Chapter 3

Designing Your Dream: Deciding on a Restaurant Concept

"Victory is sweetest when you've known defeat." -
Malcolm Forbes

You have made the decision to open your own restaurant. It's an exciting time, and the first step is to choose your restaurant concept. This is very important, because it will determine everything else about your new venture! Be sure that the restaurant you design is based on your passion for the business. This is the best way to ensure that you do not run out of steam when you run into the occasional challenge.

If you are planning to open a franchise, you will not need to worry about how your restaurant looks. That will already be decided, along with the menu and the advertising practices. Owning an independent restaurant is more demanding in the sense that it requires you to design everything on your own.

Keep in mind that each addition to your décor will cost money. As you plan the type of restaurant you want to run, make a list of everything that you will need to buy in order to bring your vision to life. Sometimes, you can work with local individuals and businesses to help you create the look of your restaurant for a much lower cost than you would pay for the same services from national companies. This can help you achieve the look you want for a lower price. Be aware that the cost will definitely be different for each type of restaurant.

Do you want your restaurant to be an intimate place that seats only a few patrons? A niche restaurant focusing on one cuisine may be the best option. If you would rather have a place that suits large crowds of people, you might want to go with a restaurant with broad appeal and a varied menu so there is something for everyone.

There are plenty of restaurant concepts to choose from, so let's examine a few of the most common options. The first style is the fast food franchise. One of the advantages of a franchise is that it is already proven to work. The cost of opening a franchise restaurant is going to be higher than the cost of opening a one of a kind restaurant. Franchises may serve hamburgers, chicken, or foreign cuisine.

What do you see when you think about how your perfect restaurant looks? Maybe you would like to have retro posters on the walls and a relaxed atmosphere. A 1950's diner may be the right theme for you. If you prefer a more upscale, hip mood, maybe you should look into an ultra modern bistro.

Casual dining is another possibility. It tends to offer a family-friendly atmosphere and includes service from wait staff. The food is usually priced in the mid-range, and the type of food could be any kind of cuisine, from global fusion to comfort food. Fast casual dining is an offshoot of this type, but fast casual restaurants usually have disposable plates. Some fast casual restaurants differentiate themselves by offering vegetarian fare or specialty items.

A café is a type of restaurant that may have outdoor dining and pastries, coffee, and other sweets. Cafés serve light, flavorful meals, are less costly than other restaurants, and typically don't have wait staff. The café can offer hot and cold entrees. Café fare often stems from the style and cuisine of France, and it has a relaxed, elegant mood.

Fine dining is considered by many to be the epitome of the restaurant experience. The fine dining restaurant has superb food that tends to be priced on the higher end of the spectrum, and it is prepared by a chef who has extensive training and experience.

Franchise vs. Independent Restaurants

If you are still not sure if you want to own a franchise or an independent restaurant, take time to check out some of the pros and cons of each type. There are some aspects of franchise restaurants that you should know about from the beginning. For instance, a franchise is going to cost more to open because there are several fees you will have to pay: the cost of buying it, the royalties from the profit you make, and the fees you will have to pay for using the franchise marketing. Be aware that you may have to agree to a 10 year contract in order to open some franchises.

The benefits of a franchise restaurant may outweigh the negatives, though. For starters, a franchise usually has brand recognition built in. You won't be starting from scratch to build up a client base. Franchises also frequently get better deals when buying ingredients and equipment because they are members of a big group.

An independent restaurant requires a much lower startup fee, but it demands a lot of planning on the owner's part. You will have to literally build your customer base alone, without the benefit of name recognition. While you will get none of the training or marketing tools that you would get from a franchise, you will have the option of running the restaurant as you desire. The independent restaurant owner can expect a much greater return on investment because he or she is not bound to pay royalty fees. You will have complete control of everything about your restaurant, from the color of the walls to the menu style. This is the real allure of the independent restaurant for many people.

Once you know what type of restaurant you want to open, it's time to get started on the work of making your dream a reality!

How to Become a Franchisee

If you decided that you want to open your own franchise restaurant, there are a few steps you will need to take. Purchasing a franchise can take much longer than you might expect, so be prepared to have a bit of patience. Once you have picked the franchise that you want to buy, it's time to start doing some research.

You want to know everything you can about the company before you sign the dotted line. That means you need to investigate the places where the franchise has already been set up and see how it is doing. Is it growing, or remaining stagnant? It is also wise to speak with people who already own one of the franchise restaurants and find out if the business is making a healthy profit.

You also need to spend time reading everything the company provides for franchisees. You may want to consult a franchise attorney to help you understand the Uniform Franchise Offering Circular. The attorney can also help you make sense of the contract you will have to sign in order to purchase the franchise.

There are a number of fees that you will have to pay upfront. The obvious one is the purchasing cost, but there are others, including the royalty fees and the marketing fees that some companies require you to pay. Some franchises have much higher fees, and you will want to beware of companies that overcharge.

Buying a franchise is not an easy process, but things can run much more smoothly if you are knowledgeable about what you are getting into! Study the company's literature, talk to people who have been there, and be savvy about the average fees you can expect to pay. You can have a great experience and start your franchise with a minimum of stress and surprises if you are willing to do the preliminary work.

Types of Restaurants

In addition to the types of dining establishments mentioned earlier, some restaurant concepts are narrower. One of these is the barbecue joint, where you can usually find brisket, smoked meats, and simple vegetable sides. Are you interested in helping people make healthy choices about what they eat? You may want to run an organic restaurant, complete with vegetarian and vegan menu items.

A few eating establishments are growing in popularity even though they are unusual. The raw bar is one example. This kind of restaurant offers clams, mussels, and other raw seafood. Sometimes you can get chowders and other cooked entrees at a raw bar. Another interesting option is the tea room. At a tea room, customers have a variety of delicate sandwiches and sweets as well as many kinds of tea.

Do you want to bring the flavor of Italy to your restaurant? An Italian establishment with a family atmosphere is called a trattoria, while a more upscale restaurant would be referred to as a ristorante. The more authentic the recipes your Italian restaurant uses, the better! People enjoy getting to taste the cuisine of another country.

Diners are another popular option. They often provide a choice of seating between tables and the bar. Traditional diner food is usually down-home and may include milkshakes, burgers, and breakfast food. These restaurants are usually set up in small buildings and may have vintage décor for that old-fashioned feeling.

Pubs usually offer a number of beers, full menus, and some kind of snack food or appetizer. They tend to serve hearty fare, such as shepherd's pie and fried fish. Some sports bars are similar to pubs and provide a good spot for the local sports fans and players to hang out. Typical sports bars usually serve onion rings and buffalo wings, among other items.

No matter which restaurant concept interests you, take hold of it and make it your own!

Chapter 4

Location, Location, Location: Choosing a Location for Your Restaurant

*"We are told that talent creates its own opportunities. But it sometimes seems that intense desire creates not only its own opportunities, but its own talents." - **Eric Hoffer***

Now that you have decided between franchise and independent options for the concept of your restaurant, you have another decision to make. Where will you put your restaurant? The location of your dining establishment can help bring you success or contribute to the difficulty of running your business.

You may be able to use an existing building for your restaurant. You might be lucky enough to find a building that has the required space and style you need. Many restaurants began life as warehouses, strip mall vacancies, and even hotel lobbies. If you can't find a building ready to use, don't give up. Any space can be renovated over time to match more closely to your vision, and it is, of course, possible to build from the ground up.

As you study the area where you wish to start your restaurant, be sure to learn about the population base. A larger number of people will bolster your ability to make a profit week after week. You do not want to start up a fine dining establishment in a town that only has a handful of residents.

You should also find out about the competition. Is there a restaurant down the street that will compete with you for the patrons? Restaurants can and do survive in close proximity to one another, but they should usually be different enough that they attract their own demographic of customers.

The cost of property and space is another thing you will need to consider. No matter how perfect the location, it can quickly become imperfect when the cost is too high to manage. Be sure that you know what is reasonable for each area you are interested in.

The location is not necessarily a make or break aspect of your restaurant, but it is very important. Knowing a few facts about the surrounding area where you want to have your restaurant can help you make the most of your location.

Finding the Perfect Location

You probably have dreams of exactly how your restaurant will look and where it will be. Perhaps it should be on the beach, nestled between surf shops and boat rental stores. Maybe your restaurant belongs in a cozy neighborhood, or it might look more at home on a busy downtown street.

If you see a place that looks right, take time out to visit at the hours when your restaurant will be open. Sometimes the building that looks so hip in the afternoon can look downright scary at night. You want the surroundings to welcome patrons in before they ever set foot in your restaurant. Keep an eye out for the amount of people that pass your potential restaurant throughout the day, including pedestrians, cyclists, and drivers.

Before you sign on a lease, find out if your landlord will consider investing in your business. Many landlords enjoy having restaurants on their property because it increases traffic to their other areas and raises the value for all of it. Sometimes a landlord will give you a few months of rent for free as you set up. They do this because they expect to gain from the presence of your restaurant.

You should keep a sharp eye out for any changes that will have to be made to the building before you can open. Too many renovations may turn your potentially perfect location into a nightmare. Plumbing, electric, and kitchen safety details will need to be worked out long before you open your doors to hungry clients! To make sure you stay within the laws governing the food industries, you may want to find a consultant who is familiar with the zoning laws in your county.

No matter what your perfect location looks like, it will be uniquely yours. It can be achieved with hard work and some research.

How to Determine Population Base

One of the things you will need to know before choosing a location is how to determine the population base. Learning this ahead of time can help you pinpoint exactly where you should build your restaurant.

Many companies choose to do a site survey, but this can cost tens of thousands of dollars. A better option is to use the documentation that is already there for you! Get in touch with the local Small Business Administration to find people who are willing to help independent restaurant owners. City councils probably have data on how the economy is doing, and they will likely be happy to share that information with someone who is going to bring new business to their area.

The population census is another way to learn about an area's demographics. You should look at the median age and income of the population and consider it as you decide on your restaurant's theme, menu, and pricing.

Another way to tell if you have a prime restaurant spot is to look at the surroundings. Is there a museum, amusement park, historical site, or bustling sports stadium close by? You can count on these types of attractions to draw people from across the country. A restaurant can thrive in the busy environment created by plenty of commerce.

You may also want to look into the unemployment rate in the area where you are considering opening a restaurant. If there are too many people struggling to find work, your restaurant may not be able to make a profit. An unemployment rate that is above 4% is reason to be extremely cautious about setting up a restaurant in that area.

If you want your new restaurant to reach its full potential, take the time to study the population base first! Learn who will be visiting the area and how much they will be likely to want to spend.

How to Negotiate a Lease

Unless you have piles of money to play with, you will probably end up needing to lease the building for your restaurant. Many people are afraid of the process of negotiating a lease, but it does not have to be scary or difficult. There are a few rules you can follow to make this a simple experience.

First of all, the landlord may be willing to work with you to make it easier for you to succeed. If you are leasing in a building or area that has relatively few businesses, the landlord might be so eager to get a business in there that he or she will let you have the first few months at no charge.

You may be able to negotiate an extremely low rent fee at the beginning of your lease and then allow it to increase over time. This is called pro-rated rent. You may also have the advantage if you end up doing major work on the building. If there are repairs that have to be made and you do them, the landlord may give you a better deal on the rent.

Be extremely cautious about signing a lease that requires you to rent the space for a long time. In the unfortunate event of your restaurant failing, you could be required to pay for many months during which you are not even using the space. Negotiate with the landlord to see if he or she will lease for a couple months at a time.

Negotiating a lease is one of the final steps you take before you get into the fun part of bringing your dream to life! Take this process seriously and make sure you get the most out of your rented space. It will be one of the big bills you have to pay each month, so it needs to be worth it.

Analyzing the Competition in Your Area

As you plan out your restaurant's theme, pricing, and menu, it is vital that you check out the competition in your area. This is important for several reasons.

To start with, you need to know how the other restaurant owners have made it. If possible, talk to them about what they have done in order to succeed. They may have helpful advice about how to best take advantage of the area's unique strengths. You can also learn a lot from the mistakes of restaurants that have gone before you.

There are different kinds of competition in your restaurant's area of influence. Some of them are direct competitors. These are restaurants that serve food that is similar in price and style to your food. Indirect competitors are restaurants that are around you, but serve completely different cuisine and target a different demographic.

Find out as much as possible about the way the competition markets to potential clients. You may want to explore the vendors that other restaurants use in order to get the most economical deal available. Pay special attention to anything that the competition does that seems to wow the customers and see if you can incorporate those tactics into your own restaurant.

Take time to explore the kinds of food and the quality that is served by the restaurants that surround you. Will your restaurant be able to compete? Take care to learn about the strong points and the weak points of your competition. You might be able to excel in areas where other restaurants have struggled.

Analyzing the competition is the first step toward dominating the restaurant scene. However, you should also be aware of the special things that set your restaurant apart from the rest. This can help your restaurant gain an edge and draw in patrons.

Chapter 5

Restaurant Business Planning: Writing a Restaurant Business Plan

*"We don't grow unless we take risks. Any successful company is riddled with failures." - **James E. Burke***

Once you have researched your competition and the population base, it is time to write a solid business plan. No restaurant can survive without a good business plan. You need to be willing to spend as much time as it takes in order to put together a plan for the restaurant you want to open. Why is this so vital?

To begin with, you need to create a business plan so you will have a roadmap to follow. Opening a restaurant is hard work, and it will only be more difficult if you are not certain about what you want to achieve in the long run. A good business plan can help you determine what steps you need to take to get to the level of success you want.

You will also gain a lot of understanding of the restaurant industry. Not only will you learn about the costs of running a restaurant, you will become better educated about your restaurant's surroundings.
You'll learn even more about the competition, the art of marketing, the food service laws, and applicable fees.

You will also need a business plan so that you can present it to those who may wish to invest in your restaurant. Most restaurant owners need to get outside funding in order to finance their venture, and this is not an easy thing to accomplish.

Banks will definitely want to see a well-written, detailed business plan before they feel comfortable loaning you money for starting a restaurant. If you ask other local businesses (or even individuals) to consider donating for repairs, equipment, and other costs, it will help them say yes if you have a business plan you can present.

Writing a business plan for your restaurant does not have to be arduous. It can actually help you focus on your goals. This chapter will guide you through the process of writing the perfect business plan.

Even if you are not naturally good at writing, you can create a good restaurant business plan. Keep in mind that you do not have to include every detail in your plan. Just give enough information to explain your goals and projections for the restaurant of your dreams.

If you feel that you simply cannot write the plan yourself, you may want to hire someone to do it for you, or enlist the help of a friend who is willing to volunteer. Be sure to spend time explaining exactly what you want included in the business plan and look it over for accuracy.

This is where all the research you did will pay off. You will need to have hard data for your business plan, so if you have not gathered enough info on the competition, the market, and the population base, it would be wise to hold off on the business plan until you have those numbers in hand.

However, assuming you have already done all the necessary legwork, it is time to sit down and think about the logistics of running a restaurant. Your business plan can help you decide what is important to you in the first several months to a year of owning a restaurant.

Even after your funds have been secured and your restaurant is open for business, you should take the time to look at the business plan. It can help remind you of what your initial plans were and keep you from veering off course. A great business plan is flexible enough to change over time with your restaurant. Our next section will help you learn the basic form to use when writing the restaurant business plan.

Basic Business Plan Outline

Be sure that you use the preferred form for business plans. Begin your plan with an executive summary. This part should tell your readers what your restaurant will be named, where it will be, and the style it will have. You should write in a way that will draw your readers in and make them feel familiar with your restaurant. They should be able to picture the restaurant's theme from your executive summary.

This is also the part where you promote yourself as a competent restaurant owner. You need to prove that you have the ability to manage a restaurant. Whether you have decades of experience in the kitchen or have just started out, you need to have enough enthusiasm and confidence that your readers will feel confident in you.

The company description comes next. It offers a few more details about the restaurant, including the information on the competition that you gathered earlier.

The business plan should then move on to market analysis. In this part of your plan, you should explain the nitty-gritty of your target demographic. Tell the reader why your restaurant, and not the competition, will bring in patrons. Your competition should be acknowledged, and you should explain how you plan to overcome the other restaurants in the area. You should also include marketing information, including the ways you plan to grab the attention of potential clients.

Continue with the business operation section of the business plan. Explain the number of people you want to employ, your hours of operation, and the benefits of your restaurant's location.

Management and ownership comes next. Write down who will do which jobs, and what positions you may hire for. If you are going to manage everything, write about how you are qualified for such a big undertaking.

Once you have covered all that, it is time to get down to the question of funding. Your business plan translates into real world money, and you need to have a comprehensive list of the expenses you expect to incur as well as the profit you expect to make. You should even point out the risks involved and include a plan to handle those risks.

Financial Projections for Restaurants

Your business plan needs to include financial projections. This will allow your potential investors to see where you envision your restaurant going in the next several months to a year. If you want to convince the banks to loan you money, you will definitely want to have some solid financial projections.

Since your restaurant will be brand new, you will not be able to look at your previous sales to project future business. How can you make these financial projections when you don't know what will happen in the upcoming months?

The answer lies in the market analysis you have already conducted. The data you collected about who your customers will be, how much they are likely to want to spend, and how much business you can expect to get will be combined with the costs of running a restaurant. Every expense, from repairs to the rent to a liquor license, should be included in the financial projection part of your plan.

The great benefit of writing financial projections is that it helps you to realistically predict how much of a profit you can make over time. If you find that the outflow of money is going to outweigh the inflow, you will need to make some changes in order to make your venture financially sound.

You will need to estimate the average number of patrons you can expect to serve each day and also the average amount of money each patron will spend. This will help you discover your average sales. Keep in mind that many restaurants have peak seasons. Certain days of the week tend to be busier, as well. Take a look at restaurants that are similar to your own in order to get a good ballpark figure for your sales projection.

If you are writing a 12-month financial projection, you need to find the amount of your potential annual sales. Start by writing down the number of weeks for the off-season (when the fewest customers come in), the middle-season, and the peak season.

Look at your competition and make an educated guess about the amount of sales you will make each day. Take that number and use it to find the weekly amount of sales. Do this for all three seasons. Next, take the sales projections for one week in a season and multiply it times the number of weeks in that same season. Do this for the other two seasons, add the resulting numbers together, and you will have a 12-month financial projection!

Make sure that you include a break even analysis in the financial segment of your business plan. This is the part that demonstrates the point where your costs are matched by your revenues. Pay close attention to the difference between fixed costs and variable costs.
Fixed costs will not change. You could sell five meals or fifty and the cost would be the same. Everything you have to pay for upfront before opening day will be a fixed cost. This includes your lease, any equipment you buy, and the fees you pay to get licensed in the food industry.

Variable costs can change over time. They stem from items you buy that are covered by the amount for which you sell them.

Your break even analysis should be done according to this formula: subtract the variable costs from the unit prices, then divide the fixed costs by this number. You have the break-even number you will need in order to know when your restaurant is making a profit and when something needs to change!

Remember, a 12-month financial projection is not set in stone. Bankers and investors do not expect it to be an airtight guarantee that you will make those exact figures. However, the thought that goes into a financial projection can help show them that you have a good chance of succeeding.

Budgeting Your Restaurant

Once you have finished your financial projection, you will need to start budgeting your restaurant. These tips will help you succeed as you decide where to spend each penny of your budget!

First of all, keep a close eye on food cost. The ingredients you buy each week can add up, and you have to be vigilant to make sure that you are profiting. Take common sense measures to ensure that you do not end up wasting food, such as storing it where it will not go bad and preparing only as much ahead of time as necessary.

Your marketing budget is an area where you need to be careful. It is easy to get caught up in the idea of running a marketing blitz that may or may not work! Choose only the marketing strategies that can be tested and measured. A measurable marketing technique could be a coupon for a discounted meal or a free dessert. Ads are only measurable if you have some way to know which customers came in due to the ads.

You should always, always know the balance of cash you have at the end of each business day. This is so vital that it is worth hiring someone to handle if you won't be able to keep up with it. Keeping an eye on your cash flow will help you make wise choices about staffing, marketing, and menu pricing.

Try to always project your cash balance 6 months ahead. This will help you be prepared and give you some spending guidelines. It can also show you the places where costs tend to get out of hand. Keep your financial projections updated as much as possible, and use those numbers to your advantage.

Now that the financial details have been considered, it's time to dive into the fun of honing the theme of your restaurant!

Chapter 6

Refining Your Restaurant Concept

"We owe a lot to Thomas Edison - if it wasn't for him, we'd be watching television by candlelight." - **Milton Berle**

If you don't have a clear view of what you want your restaurant to look like and become over the next several months, it's time to do some thinking on that subject! You probably already have a few things decided, like what kind of food you will serve. However, your restaurant concept is much more than the content of your menu.

There are a few questions you should ask yourself as you refine the idea of your restaurant that is already in your head. For example, is your restaurant going to be able to grow? Can you replicate your restaurant later on, if you choose?

Does your restaurant have the ability to distinguish itself from the many competing restaurants nearby? You want to have a dining establishment that grabs the attention of your potential customers. Sometimes this can be accomplished by skillfully stepping into a niche that is open. An organic deli is one example of a niche restaurant that could become quite successful. Be sure that your restaurant doesn't just follow the trends, but uses current methods in a way that will last!

Even if you are confident in your restaurant concept, keep an open mind during the first couple of months of operation. If you are a brand new restaurant owner and manager, you will face numerous surprises as you learn to run the business. Be vigilant about coaching your staff and any assistant management. Be willing to make changes if necessary in order to make procedures as smooth as possible.

If you find that working on the restaurant concept is getting the best of you, it may be wise to consult a professional restaurant developer who can help you bring about your vision. Look for dedicated business consultants who are veterans of the restaurant industry and who are willing to listen to your input. After all, this is your restaurant!

Writing the Menu

Once you have the concept of your restaurant pinned down, you should feel more comfortable writing the menu. A good menu should be easy to read and understand. Avoid long, involved descriptions of your menu items. However, the descriptions should make your patrons eager to taste what you're serving. They should clearly identify any ingredients that are likely to be unfamiliar.

The style of your menu should mesh well with the theme of your restaurant. Choose fonts that are easy to read, even for older guests. The menu should be uncluttered, although there are many options for the layout. Ethnic restaurant menus often feature the colors that are associated with the country's flag.

Make sure to know which items are going to be the main draw. Why should patrons come to your restaurant instead of the one down the street? What are you serving that they can't find anywhere else? Focus on your strengths. At the same time, try to include enough options so that everyone can find something to eat. Every restaurant theme, from barbecue to French country cuisine, has its own classics that can be enjoyed by those who want something familiar.

You may want to arrange your menu according to the course. Salads, appetizers, and soups should come early in the menu, followed by the entrees, sides, and desserts. Add a noticeable icon any special deals, healthy options, or vegetarian dishes to help your guests decide what to order.

You can create separate lunch and dinner menus to keep things simple for your patrons. If you want to change up the menu once in a while, try writing special menus for holidays or write a slightly different menu for each season.

No matter what your restaurant's theme, keep it in mind as you create the perfect menu! The theme should always be your roadmap.

How to Price Your Menu

As you start pricing your menu, it is crucial that you study the restaurants that are competing with you. The cost of your food should not be drastically higher or lower than that of the competition. If you have an item that is significantly more expensive than a similar dish at a competing restaurant, make sure that it is special enough to warrant the extra dollars patrons will spend.

Another technique to help you price your menu is to examine how much you pay for each unit of food. Are you charging enough to make a profit? The price that guests pay not only has to cover the food itself, it also needs to contribute to the costs of running the restaurant! On top of that, you want to make a profit from the business. This is why many restaurants markup their food by as much as 35%.

The menu you have created should have wiggle room for when food prices change. This means you need to include a range of prices. Do not build your entire menu on only expensive dishes or their cheaper counterparts. The best course of action is to have balance. This can ease the cash crunch when your restaurant goes through the inevitable ups and downs of a changing market.

Keep a close eye on how much food is being served. Portion control is vital to making a steady profit. You should ensure that each dish only has the amount of food that it should. This can help you avoid wasting food or charging too little for a large dish. Every piece of food that goes out should be measured and consistent.

Portion control, knowledge of the competition, and a balance of high price and low price items can help you get the most out of your menu pricing. If you follow these simple steps, you can create a menu that will make your patrons want to return again and again.

Menu Design

Once you have decided on the dishes your restaurant will serve and know how you will price those items, you will need to work on designing your menu. The look of your menu is very important. It should fit in with the restaurant as a whole. Avoid colors that clash with your décor, taking into consideration the paint on the walls and the colors associated with the cuisine of your choice. For instance, diners are often decorated with pastel green and pink shades, while Mexican restaurants generally boast warm earth tones.

Photographs of the food are appropriate for some restaurants, such as casual dining. Family-oriented restaurants and franchises often use pictures on the menus to encourage patrons to buy certain items. However, photos are not always helpful. The more formal restaurants avoid using pictures, as it takes away from the elegance of the menu.

The format of your menu may be the front and back of a single page, a folding page with three panels, or even a multi-page book. The pages should be laminated or placed in plastic sleeves. This will make them easy to wipe free of food and drink spills and will help your restaurant maintain an air of cleanliness.

If you are not confident in your formatting skills, there are numerous services that can help you design your menu. Some of these services are quite reasonably priced. You can also create menus using templates that are available on the web, although these templates should be carefully scrutinized to make sure they give your menu a professional appearance.

Finally, be confident in your restaurant's theme. Let the excitement you feel for your dishes show in the menu itself with irresistible descriptions and a beautiful format! Your patrons should read your menu and feel like they would enjoy anything listed on it.

Tips for Writing a Restaurant Menu

In case you still want a little more guidance on writing your menu, here are a few final tips before we move on to the topic of running the restaurant. First of all, consider what kind of restaurant you are managing. This should tell you a few things about how to complete a perfect menu.

For example, nearly every patron of a themed restaurant comes with some preconceptions about what the menu will include. An Italian restaurant will usually serve a number of familiar pasta dishes, a few salads, and maybe even pizza. However, there is also room to add some Italian dishes that might not be as familiar to guests. Mexican restaurants tend to serve fajitas, rice, enchiladas, and tacos – but some dining establishments also serve barbecued goat and other dishes that are equally different! A menu should have a balance between the classic dishes and the specialty options in order to keep everyone happy.

If you are going to serve breakfast, lunch, and dinner, you will have to decide if you want to put all three meals on one menu. Many restaurants offer separate lunch and dinner menus, and a few even have a dessert menu. Wine lists can also be a great addition to your restaurant, and they can be written on the same menu or kept separate.

If you run a somewhat casual restaurant, you may want to write the specials down on a chalkboard each day. This can catch a patron's eye as he or she walks in the door and encourage the purchase of your special dish. This technique will not work for every style of restaurant. It could be very useful for bar and grill restaurants, cafes, and even bakeries.

Now that we've walked you through writing your menu, it's time to move on to the management of your restaurant!

Chapter 7

How to Run Your Restaurant

*"We were born to succeed, not to fail." - **Henry David Thoreau***

This chapter will help you understand the many tasks you will be called upon to fulfill as a restaurant owner. While starting your restaurant is exciting, and writing the menu was probably a lot of fun, you may feel overwhelmed by the unknown difficulties of being the owner and manager. After you finish reading this chapter, you should feel much more confident and have a grasp on what you need to do as the owner.

You will be responsible for everything that happens in your restaurant. However, that does not mean that you have to do everything by yourself! It simply means that you need to delegate tasks with care. You must have confidence that you have chosen the right people to do those jobs. The next section will give you more detail about how to find staff that will be an asset to your business.

As the owner, you will need to be competent with handling people's problems. This means using good listening skills, especially when your staff is talking! Your staff can often give you solid advice, particularly if they have already been in the food industry for years. You will also need to be willing to hear the complaints and suggestions of customers.

After all, they are the ones who are keeping your restaurant in business. Including some way for guests to have input on your service and food can help you gain the insight you need. This could take the form of a suggestion box for a casual restaurant or an online review form for a more upscale eatery.

However, the customer is not always right. Some people will attempt to take advantage of you simply because they assume you don't know that ropes. Be fair and remain calm even when faced with rude, loud guests.

Find out what needs to happen on your end each day and make those tasks your priority. You can't do it all, so make sure that everything you add to your job checklist for the day is necessary.

Restaurant owners should plan on rising early each day, whether or not they choose to serve breakfast. Many delivery trucks run in the morning, and they will be bringing you the food, paper supplies, and other necessities for the day. If you are serving lunch, be sure to include menu items that can be created during the typical lunch hour.

Each evening will probably bring a dinner rush. Keep in mind that your patrons are hoping to have a calm, enjoyable meal and make sure that any problems have been handled before they arrive. This includes finding replacements or delegating work when a waiter or cook is on vacation or ill. You should also make sure that all your wait staff are aware of the dishes that are specials that day.

A great restaurant owner and manager is one that is accessible. You should make regular appearances in your restaurant. One action that always makes a great impression is to check up on how patrons are enjoying their food. Asking about their experience can not only make you look like a top-notch manager, it can help you spot potential problems before they turn into big issues. The opinions of your patrons can also help you see where you are doing things right in this new venture!

The rest of this chapter is devoted to the tricks of the trade. You will learn about using a POS system, hiring staff for various positions, and the benefits of leasing kitchen equipment rather than buying it outright. Our next topic will help you learn all about the kitchen staff positions you will need to fill before the grand opening of your restaurant.

Staffing Your Restaurant

Your restaurant can't run with only one person at the wheel! You need to hire staff to take care of the tasks you can't accomplish. There are some staff positions that are necessary for every restaurant.

The dishwasher is the first person you should hire. He or she needs to be willing to wash dishes and clean and do any other odd jobs that come up in the course of the day. This is a job that requires a lot of hard work, and you should treat your dishwasher well! A good dishwasher can be promoted within your restaurant.

A prep cook does the often thankless food tasks: chopping vegetables, making dough ahead of time, and putting together soups. These jobs are extremely important, even though prep cooks usually do not get much credit. They create the base flavors from which the rest of the food will be cooked. Don't discount the work the prep cook performs each day.

A line cook is responsible for the next step in the process. The term "line cook" comes from the line of your kitchen stations. A line cook is going to be taking care of one kind of cooking, whether it is sautéing, frying, or some other style. Many prep cooks are going to want to work up to line cook positions.

The sous chef works directly under the chef. He runs the restaurant any time when the chef is unable to do so. Sous chefs tend to train the other cooks, and some kitchens have more than one sous chef.

Wait staff are also necessary parts of your restaurant. The wait staff should be friendly and able to interact well with all personality types! You will need to have enough wait staff to go around even on the busiest of nights.

Hiring for Front of the House

The front of the house positions are the ones that your patrons will see. They will come in contact with your front of house staff as soon as they come in the door. There are some basic positions that you will need to fill for the front of house work. This section will teach you what those jobs are and what to look for when hiring for them.

The first person your patrons will see is probably going to be the host or hostess. This position requires someone who loves to meet people and interact with them. A host will be in charge of seating the patrons and making them feel comfortable. Anyone can do this job with the right attitude. Multi-taskers often thrive in this position.

If you have a bar in your restaurant, a bartender is a necessary person. This job demands someone who is trustworthy with money. He or she should know how to make numerous mixed drinks and be well-versed in knowledge about various liquors.

Busboys can be a valuable addition to your restaurant. This is a job for the eager jack-of-all-trades. It often consists of moving back and forth from the back of the house to the front while cleaning tables, running errands for swamped kitchen staff, and maybe even cooking simple dishes when the cooks get behind.

The cashiers should be people you can trust. They are going to be handling the majority of your money. Sometimes, the wait staff is in charge of taking care of the payments and giving the patrons their receipts. The wait staff needs to be aware of the kind of food they will be describing to guests, and they should also be friendly.

As you hire staff members for the front of the house positions, keep in mind how they will fit into the overall theme of your restaurant. Constantly ask yourself if the person you are considering for a job is the right fit for the position and for your restaurant. This simple question will help you build a stellar team!

Back of the House Positions

The term "back of the house" refers to the area your guests do not see. This includes the business office (if there is one), any storage areas, and the kitchen.

You may own an independent restaurant and also be the head chef. Be warned that you may want to hire a kitchen manager. This person can keep the flow of your kitchen running smoothly. He or she needs to know what your expectations are for each dish and be willing to ensure that every item goes out the way you want it. If you are not going to be the chef, you will need to employ someone for this job. A chef needs to be very knowledgeable and confident in the kitchen. He or she should also be willing to listen to your input and make changes accordingly.

Your sous chef should be dependable. He or she needs to be someone you can count on to keep the quality of your food high even when the head chef is away. A sous chef is often quite educated about the workings of a restaurant kitchen and can help your other staff learn.

Another back of the house position is that of dishwasher. Your dishwashers can easily move up to higher positions if they prove themselves to be great employees. Don't take a good dishwasher for granted!

If you have a large, upscale restaurant, you may want to hire a saucier. This person will be in charge of creating the sauces that bring that extra kick of flavor to your dishes. A saucier should be willing to work with the rest of the kitchen crew and needs to be able to stand at the stove for extended periods of time. Many sauciers start out as prep cooks who learn the necessary skills to create delicious sauces.

Equipping Your Restaurant

Once you have found your staff, you will start to see how your business will look. But your new restaurant will also need to be equipped before you are ready to open your doors for business. There are several pieces of equipment that are vital to every restaurant, and some items that will only be needed for certain types of food.

You will definitely need a refrigerator, an oven with a range, and a freezer. You may also have to get an icemaker so your patrons can count on getting a cold drink! Other equipment, such as mixing machines, double boilers, and assorted specialty items may also be needed.

Heat lamps can help you keep your food hot until it can be served. Industrial can openers will speed things along in your kitchen and guarantee a neatly opened can each time. If you are going to serve a lot of sliced vegetables, you may want to add a mandolin slicer to your inventory. These cutting tools have razor sharp blades set in a plastic handle so you can easily and quickly make uniform slices.

No matter what kind of equipment you require, there are a few tips you should know as you shop. One option is to use equipment that is known for being environmentally friendly. Green products can save you a lot of money by reducing the use of energy in your business. They can also heighten your marketability if you are presenting your restaurant as an organic, vegetarian, or earth-conscious venture.

There are several companies that lease restaurant equipment for a reasonable cost. If you are unsure about the specifics of a piece of equipment, don't be afraid to ask! A good company will be happy to help you find items in the size and style you are looking for.

Why You Need a POS System

A POS system is a "point of sale" system that can help you know exactly where the money is coming from. It is a computer program that can give you the information you need about the cash flow of your business. A POS system is crucial because you will have too many customers to keep up with every purchase.

While you should hire trustworthy staff members, there is always the possibility that someone could try to cheat you or steal money from the company. Once you have a POS system, it can not only deter staff members from skimming money off the top of their sales, but it can help you know when this is happening.

A POS system can double as a credit card processor, which means that these sales are safer for both sides of the transaction. As more and more people become fearful of identity theft, this is a great benefit.

Any orders that are entered into the POS system will automatically be sent to be printed through your computer system. The POS system can also help you manage your business and take care of your accounting. It can write a profit and loss statement and even keep track of the sales tax that you have been charged.

The POS system will simplify your life immensely just by recording each sale. If you are running a franchise or are opening a restaurant that is going to be mid-sized to large, you must get a POS system. It can help you avoid staying overtime trying to figure out how much you made each day and whether or not there has been a mistake or a theft.

A POS system is a tool that can make your job much easier. You will have plenty to do without having to balance the books each day. Pay the initial fee for one of these systems and you will enjoy the benefits for years to come!

Why You Should Lease Equipment Instead of Buying It

There are a few clear benefits to leasing equipment instead of buying it. This section will teach you the reasons behind our suggestion that you lease all equipment.

To start with, it is a sad fact that not every restaurant succeeds. If you find that you need to sell your restaurant or simply close it down, you do not want to be stuck with tons of kitchen equipment, too. Leasing the equipment you need is one sure way to know that you will not be carrying an extra burden if the worst happens to your restaurant.

You will also be paying huge amounts of money if you decide to purchase all your equipment at the beginning of your new venture. Getting the equipment on lease is a much less costly way to outfit your kitchen. Nearly every piece of heavy equipment can be leased, from the range to the refrigerator. When you come to the end of the lease, you can easily get a new item to replace the old one.

You can also use the lease option to avoid buying too many items at once! It's easy to get overenthusiastic about buying equipment, and you could end up purchasing equipment that your restaurant may not even need. Make sure that every single piece of equipment that you are considering is truly necessary, and lease it just in case you discover that you don't need it down the road.

As you expand, you should continue leasing your equipment. The company you lease from could come under new management or put different guidelines into effect, and you should always be able to change providers. An added benefit is that you are not going to have to fix leased equipment when it breaks! The company will have to repair it.

Buying equipment is unnecessary with all the great companies out there which are willing to lease you the same items.

Chapter 8

Conclusion & Bonus Materials

"Whatever you vividly imagine, ardently desire, sincerely believe, and enthusiastically act upon... must inevitably come to pass!" - **Paul J. Meyer**

Conclusion

Now that you have come nearly to the end of the book, you should feel much more confident in your ability to start a restaurant. You know that it will be a tough, demanding job, but it is one you will love doing! In fact, you can't imagine any other job you would rather have than that of restaurant owner. You've learned a lot in the past seven chapters, and in this one, we have a few final reminders for you.

Keep in mind that opening a restaurant isn't a game. It's a lot of work, and your days will start early and end late. You have a number of decisions to make if you haven't already done so.

For instance, will you manage the restaurant yourself, or hire a manager? Will you be in the kitchen, fulfilling the role of chef? Consider the amount of capital you have as well as your own need for relaxation time as you make staffing choices. Your kitchen will need several staff positions filled, but hire only the number of staff members you can afford.

If you have a great concept all planned out, congratulations! You are well on your way to bringing that vision to life as a restaurant. If you keep the suggestions for concept and menu design in mind as you work, you will create a restaurant that draws your patrons in with its atmosphere and originality.

Finally, be confident! You have come this far – now go out and meet the challenges head on. Whether those challenges come from people who don't believe in your ideas, financial institutions that are reluctant to part with funds, or even your own anxieties, you have the passion to defeat them.

The rest of the book is devoted to bonus materials on the topics already covered. Enjoy the tips and use them to your advantage as you begin building your restaurant!

How To Open a Restaurant

You will need to have some aspects of your restaurant in place before you open your doors for the public. The next sections of this chapter will give you advice on how to handle each of those parts of restaurant ownership.

Be prepared to find funding from different sources. You will probably need to get a loan from the bank in order to start leasing your space. You should also be willing to seek out alternative ways of getting the money you need. Investors, small companies, and even individuals will sometimes offer funds to worthy business ventures. Take your stellar business plan with you and as for the cash you need. Be sure to point out the benefits your investors will gain as your restaurant grows.

Take time to solidify your restaurant's theme. Whether you are eager to make a down-home casual restaurant or one that is elegant and upper-class, knowing your theme is vital. Sometimes, atmosphere is enough to set your restaurant apart from the others crowding the market.

Speaking of competition, you need to be aware of who is competing with you, directly and indirectly. Study the other restaurants in your area, find out who goes to them and what is served. Find out everything you can about how the owners do business so you can learn from their victories and mistakes.

Your level of commitment to opening the restaurant of your dreams is what will truly make it or break it. The most ambitious concept can flounder when an owner is half-hearted in the attempt to bring it to life, while a humble eatery can be lifted to greatness when it is executed with confidence.

Remember, the end result of all your hard work will be a brand new restaurant, ready to offer people amazing food and personal service. It will be worth it!

How to Write a Restaurant Business Plan

As you prepare to approach businesses and banks with your request for loans or investment funds, you need to have a great business plan ready. The people you are speaking to should get a feel for your restaurant's theme just by reading your plan. Include the name and where you are planning to open the restaurant.

Your business plan needs to include sales projections for the year. Be sure to keep in mind the different sales you can expect during peak season, off-season, and mid-season. Tell your potential investors about your strengths as a manager and owner. Talk about any culinary education that you have acquired over the years. Point out the ways the bank will benefit from your business over time, and lay out a clear plan for how and when you intend to pay off your loan.

Include your long-term and short-term goals in the business plan so investors can get an idea of how you plan to increase your profit and theirs, if applicable. Are you hoping to expand your restaurant once you get your feet on the ground? Put that in writing so they can see your vision and ambition.

Be honest about the competition you will be dealing with. Tell them how you plan to overcome these challenges. If you already have business relationships with other restaurants, food companies, or equipment dealers, mention these in your business plan.

Be sure to write about the team you plan to hire. If you already know who is going to be on your kitchen crew, explain why they are the right choices and how they will be an asset to your business. Include information on what you plan to pay for salaries, including your own if you are going to be the manager of your restaurant.

Detail the kinds of insurance you plan to get to cover unexpected issues. This will help the banks and investors feel confident that you are doing everything you can to responsibly create a restaurant that will succeed.

How to Advertise An Independent Restaurant

One of the challenges of running an independent restaurant is that of advertising. Franchises come with marketing plans ready-made. In fact, some franchises include marketing in their fees. As an independent restaurant owner, you will be on your own as far as advertising goes.

As you plan your budget, keep in mind that it will need to include advertising costs. Make it a priority to put some money aside each quarter for promoting your restaurant. The amount of advertising you can do will be determined by the amount of money you have. Sometimes, you can offer free meals to advertising companies in exchange for running your ad.

Your local paper is a great place to start advertising. You should look into the demographics that usually buy and read the paper and decide if it is the right venue for your restaurant. Most newspapers and other local magazines offer different amounts of advertising space, so you should be able to find an ad that will fit into your budget. As your restaurant grows, you can expand the amount of advertising you do to include larger ads.

Another great option is to find a high traffic area and start some outdoor advertising. Many large cities have digital billboards. The companies who have these boards will allow you to buy a certain number of views each day. The packages can be quite affordable and effective.

You can also advertise online. Contact websites that feature local restaurants and request that they add your restaurant to their database. You can even set up your own website to promote the restaurant. If you tie your website in with a promotional deal, you can make an even bigger impression on your potential clients.

Advertising an independent restaurant tends to give you more freedom than you would have with a franchise restaurant. Enjoy exploring all the ways you get to promote your new venture!

How to Manage a Restaurant

If you are managing your restaurant, you are the one in charge of everything that happens in your company. A good manager will be comfortable dealing with people from all walks of life. You will need to be able to relate not only the clients, but also to the kitchen crew and other employees in your restaurant.

Take time to speak with patrons when you can. They will feel a stronger connection to your restaurant if they see you as the face of the restaurant. You should also be able to deal fairly and calmly with the occasional patron who wants to cause a problem. One of your strongest qualities should be that of being a good listener. If you are not naturally good at listening,

As a manager, you will also need to be comfortable planning out your restaurant. The months ahead should be planned for and include clear goals for your business and your employees. Training your employees is very important and it can help your staff work together more easily.

You will need to keep a close eye on the financial side of the business, as well. At the end of the day, if someone has to go without a paycheck, it will be you! You need to use the business plan that you wrote to help you stay on track with spending. Avoid buying pricey equipment by leasing as many items as possible.

Finally, be realistic about the amount of time you are going to be spending in the restaurant each day. Accept that your mornings will likely start earlier than those of most people, and that your nights will be busy due to patrons! Set aside time after lunch and before the dinner rush to relax and maybe even catch a few winks. This little commitment to yourself can pay off by allowing you to face each evening's business well-rested and happy.

How to Make a Restaurant Menu

Your menu will spring directly from the concept of your restaurant. In fact, the theme of your dining establishment may dictate quite a few of your menu items. For those who want to stick to the classics for their theme, making a menu may be fairly simple.

For example, a casual restaurant that focuses on home cooking will probably have chicken fried steak, mashed potatoes, and gravy. Desserts will probably be along the lines of apple crumble and lemon meringue pie. A restaurant that serves familiar food can't just settle for the mundane, though; you need to have a few dishes that really stand out, either by putting a new twist on a classic recipe or by being the absolute best version of that standard dish.

Niche restaurants have a little more freedom. If you run a fusion restaurant, you will constantly be striving for the newest, tastiest combinations of ingredients. If you have a theme that allows you to play around with unconventional ingredients, make the most of them! You may have the only restaurant in town that serves that particular food.

However, don't lose sight of the fact that being too adventurous can give some potential customers reason to look elsewhere. Try to include enough classic, crowd-pleasing dishes to allow everyone the chance to enjoy your restaurant.

As you plan your menu, you should also take into consideration the way patrons will read it. Try to structure the menu in a way that makes sense –

starting with breakfast, moving on to lunch, salads, soups, dinner, and dessert. It is also acceptable to offer a separate wine list or put the dessert on its own menu.

If you have so many ideas that you can't fit them all onto your regular menu, you still have options! You can create holiday menus or seasonal menus that give patrons something different to look forward to and allow you to include all the dishes you can dream up.

For more helpful information on Starting a Restaurant join our mailing list, by simply emailing us at
startarestauran@aweber.com

How to Price Restaurant Menu Items

The process of pricing menu items can cause some restaurant owners to stress out. Are you making a profit from your dishes? Is your cost too high for the area your restaurant serves? Fortunately, there are several ways to make sure that you are pricing your dishes correctly.

Most restaurants will add 30-35% to the cost of their food to find the price. This will help cover the item's actual cost, the salaries for the kitchen staff, and other overhead. Every bill you have will be paid for by the money from selling dishes, so this markup isn't as generous as it may sound. In fact, you will probably see only very small amounts of profit at first. As your restaurant grows, your profit will, as well.

Another aspect of menu pricing that you should consider is the demographic you are serving. Some niche restaurants can charge more because they have a unique atmosphere. Urban restaurants can usually get by with charging higher prices for their food than their rural counterparts. However, even in the city you will need to know the median income of your patrons. This information will come from the research you did when deciding on your location.

It might be a good idea to consider the menu prices you are planning to charge as you look for a place to set up your restaurant. If the ingredients of your dishes are expensive, you will need to look for a demographic that will support the marked up price of the items. If your dishes are relatively inexpensive to create, you could choose a suburban or rural location where the rent is likely to be cheaper.

Your menu should include items that are more expensive and some that are more affordable. This will help broaden the client base to include people from both ends of the financial spectrum.

How to Start a Restaurant

Now that you've come to the end of the book, you probably have a much greater sense of what really goes into running a restaurant. As you plan to start your restaurant, it pays to keep a few things in mind.

The typical restaurant owner spends long hours working. In fact, most holidays and weekends will be devoted to the restaurant. You, as owner, will need to be able to multitask. Running a restaurant requires a variety of skills, and you will have to dabble in nearly all of them!

People skills will be invaluable as you work with staff members, bankers, vendors, and customers. You should be prepared to handle all kinds of personalities! Being cautious in your hiring process will help reduce the amount of interpersonal stress in the kitchen. Make sure that the staff members you hire have the education, experience, and integrity you want.

Budgeting is another vital part of starting a restaurant. Plan out how much you can realistically spend each month and stick to that plan as much as possible. If you find that you are falling behind because you don't have the funds, it would be a good idea to seek out loans from banks. You can also speak with other companies and ask them to invest in your restaurant. Make sure your business plan addresses any concerns as well as the ways in which your investors will gain from your restaurant's growth.

The final word of advice for you as you start this venture is to enjoy it! Your restaurant will shine if you pour into it all the passion you feel for the job. Don't be afraid to experiment with your menu, your prices, and your theme. The more you have fun at work, the more people will want to visit your restaurant. Bon appetit!

CPSIA information can be obtained at www.ICGtesting.com
Printed in the USA
LVOW05s1623190814

399900LV00020B/1261/P